The science of
Air

LIVING SCIENCE

Sarah Dann

Gareth Stevens Publishing
MILWAUKEE

For a free color catalog describing Gareth Stevens' list of high-quality books and multimedia programs, call 1-800-542-2595 (USA) or 1-800-461-9120 (Canada). Gareth Stevens Publishing's Fax: (414) 225-0377.

Library of Congress Cataloging-in-Publication Data available upon request from publisher. Fax (414) 225-0377 for the attention of the Publishing Records Department.

ISBN 0-8368-2569-1 (lib. bdg.)

This edition first published in 2000 by
Gareth Stevens Publishing
1555 North RiverCenter Drive, Suite 201
Milwaukee, WI 53212 USA

Project Co-ordinator: Meaghan Craven
Series Editor: Linda Weigl
Copy Editors: Rennay Craats and Kristen Higgins
Design and Illustration: Warren Clark and Chantelle Sales
Cover Design: Carole Knox
Layout: Lucinda Cage
Gareth Stevens Editor: Rita Reitci

Printed in Canada

1 2 3 4 5 6 7 8 9 04 03 02 01 00

Contents

What Do You Know about Air?

We are surrounded by air. Air is a necessary part of the world around us. It is made up of several invisible gases. Two of these gases are **oxygen** and **carbon dioxide**. Animals breathe the oxygen in air to stay alive.

Animals breathe more quickly when they are exercising so they can take in more oxygen.

Air is the **atmosphere**. The atmosphere is a layer of gases surrounding Earth. Earth's **gravity** pulls down on these gases and gives weight to air. Gravity keeps air from flying off into space.

Activity

Air Sayings

"He's full of hot air!" Many expressions use the word "air." How many expressions do you know? What do these expressions mean to you? Draw pictures to illustrate the expressions.

Sports, such as snowboarding, allow people to fly through the air and cheat gravity, if only for a few seconds.

The atmosphere reaches about 600 miles (960 kilometers) above Earth.

Breathing and Air

Every living thing needs air to survive. When people go up high mountains or into space, they take containers that are filled with air. Air containers allow these people to keep breathing in places that have little or no air.

Astronauts wear air packs to keep them breathing when they walk in space. There is no air in space.

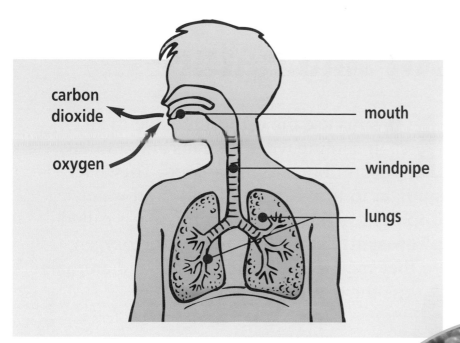

carbon dioxide

oxygen

mouth

windpipe

lungs

You need oxygen to play, run, laugh, and even to move your little finger.

When you take a deep breath, air enters your nose or mouth. It travels through your **windpipe** to your **lungs**. Inside your lungs, blood takes oxygen out of the air. Blood also puts carbon dioxide into the air that you exhale. Blood then transports oxygen throughout your body. Your body needs oxygen to burn fuels, like sugar, to produce energy.

Puzzler

Find a watch. Take a deep breath. Time how many seconds you can hold your breath. Think about swimming and breathing. Think about how breathing works. Why do you think people cannot breathe in water?

Answer: Human lungs cannot use the oxygen in water.

Air and Nature

Plants use the carbon dioxide in air, including what humans and animals contribute, to make food. They use sunlight to turn carbon dioxide and water into oxygen and sugar. This process is called **photosynthesis**. Plants release the oxygen they make into the air. People and animals use the oxygen.

Plants need humans for the carbon dioxide they provide. Without carbon dioxide, plants could not grow.

Some plants make seeds that the air carries to new places for planting. Other plants rely on air to carry their pollen from plant to plant. Plants must get pollen from other plants to make seeds that will grow into new plants.

Stand near a garden and take a deep breath. Do you smell the fresh scent of flowers? Smells are carried to our noses through the air.

Dandelions make seeds that do not need pollen to reproduce. The wind carries these seeds to other locations, where the new flowers can begin to grow.

Puzzler

What makes us sneeze? Pepper? Dust? Why do you think these things make us sneeze?

Answer: Small, unwanted particles in the nose often cause us to sneeze.

Wind

Wind is moving air. Wind can be felt as a gentle breeze or a powerful storm. A light breeze travels at 8 to 12 miles per hour (13-19 km per hour), but a hurricane can blow at more than 74 miles per hour (119 km per hour). Leaves, waves, and clouds all move because of wind.

Types of Wind

Chinook	Harmattan	Hurricane	Sea Breeze

- **Chinook**
  - Is a warm wind that blows down the eastern slopes of the Rocky Mountains in the winter
  - Can make snow melt. Can make winter seem like summer

- **Harmattan**
  - Forms over the Sahara Desert and blows west to the African coast
  - Is cool
  - Carries dust from the Sahara Desert

- **Hurricane**
  - Is a swirling storm that begins over a warm sea such as the Caribbean Sea
  - Can damage property and cause floods

- **Sea Breeze**
  - Blows from the sea to the shore
  - Occurs when warm air on land rises and cool air over the sea moves in to replace it

Every part of Earth experiences wind. There are, however, some winds that are unique to certain areas of the world. Chinooks, harmattans, hurricanes, sea breezes, tornadoes, and trade winds each inhabit certain areas.

Tornado

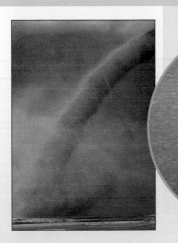

Trade Winds

- A very strong cold wind meets a very strong warm wind and they begin to spin around

- Spins along the ground in a funnel shape and destroys everything in its path

- Regular, strong winds that blow toward the equator from the northeast or southeast

- In the days of sailing ships, sailors depended on trade winds for traveling

Water in the Air

Water can travel in the air. It travels as very small particles known as **water vapor**. Water vapor is formed when water **evaporates** from oceans, lakes, and rivers. This usually happens on a hot, cloudy day. The warm temperature draws moisture from the water into the air. When the air is filled with water vapor, people say it is humid.

The rain forests around the Amazon River are very hot and humid. Areas near a beach can also be humid because of all the water vapor in the air over the ocean.

Water vapor also helps to form clouds. Wind picks up water vapor when it blows across lakes and oceans and sweeps it into the sky. The water falls back to Earth in the form of rain or snow

Some of the most spectacular rain clouds can be seen over or near water where there is a lot of water vapor.

Warm and Cold Air

Warm air is lighter than cold air. This makes air move. Warm air always rises above cold air.

Hot air balloons rise from Earth because they are filled with air that is warmer than the air outside the balloon.

Temperature differences between land and water cause mist to form on lakes and rivers.

Land heats and cools faster than water. During the day, air sitting over land is usually warmer than air sitting over water. At night, the air over land is usually cooler than the air over water. The difference in temperature makes breezes blow.

The differences in temperature between land and water affect how air moves.

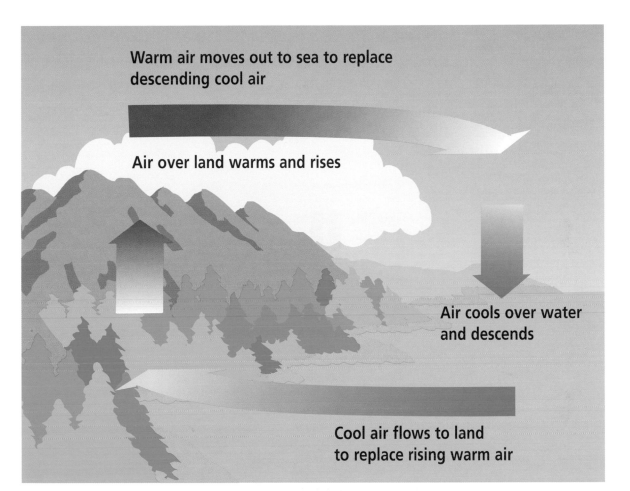

Warm air moves out to sea to replace descending cool air

Air over land warms and rises

Air cools over water and descends

Cool air flows to land to replace rising warm air

Puzzler

Some people can feel when it is going to rain. Their knees might ache or they might develop headaches. What are their bodies sensing?

Answer:
These people's bodies are reacting to the change in air pressure that happens when warm and cold air meet. People who have arthritis, a disease that affects the body's joints, seem to react the strongest.

Air Indoors

Furnaces heat buildings. Air conditioners cool buildings. Furnaces work because hot air rises above cold air. Pipes carry hot air from the furnace to rooms throughout a building. The hot air comes into a room through vents in the floor. It rises above the cold air in the room. The cold air sinks and flows back to the furnace through wall vents.

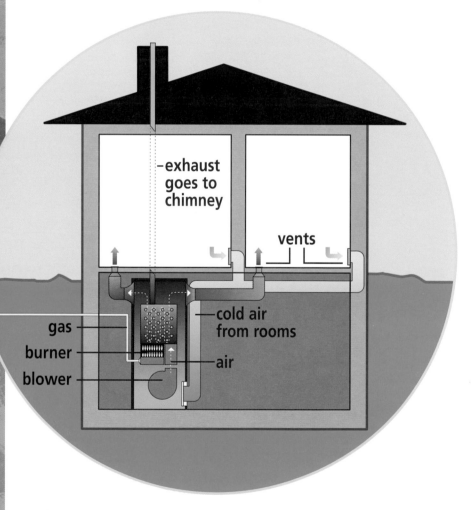

exhaust goes to chimney

vents

gas

burner

blower

cold air from rooms

air

A furnace heats the air, and vents distribute the air through the building.

Air conditioners cool hot air. They suck hot air in, cool it, and remove its moisture. Then the air conditioner blows the cooled air into the room, using a fan.

Fans move air. When it is hot, fans can cool us by moving air over our skin. The air removes water from our skin as it goes by, making us feel cooler. Fans also help keep us warm. They move hot air through our cars and homes in the winter.

Fans are used to move air around inside malls and other large buildings.

Fans do not make air cooler. They are used to move air around our bodies. The movement of air helps our bodies cool down.

Puzzler

Air conditioners keep air cool. They also clean the air of dust and pollen. Air conditioners can also cause illness. How?

Answer: If they are not cleaned and working properly, air conditioners can circulate dust and germs. Many people who work or live in air conditioned buildings can become sick this way.

Air Power

Moving air is a source of power. **Wind turbines** use moving air to create electricity. Wind turbines are tall towers. They have a wheel at the top with blades around it. Wind pushes the blades and makes the wheel spin. When the wheel spins, electrical energy is generated. Wind is a clean source of energy. Wind power does not create pollution. Nothing is burned to produce wind power.

Windmills have been used for centuries to do such things as grind grain into flour. Modern turbines generate enough power to heat many buildings.

The largest wind turbines are over 140 feet (43 meters) tall. That is as tall as a 14-story office building. There are three blades on these turbines. Each is over 65 feet (20 meters) long. That is as long as a semitrailer truck. These wind turbines can generate enough electricity each year to power over two hundred homes.

Turbines provide exciting, clean possibilities for the future of energy production.

Wind-Powered Pinwheel

Make a pinwheel that spins like a wind turbine. You will need construction paper, scissors, a strong pin, a bead, and a short wooden stick. Have an adult help you with this activity.

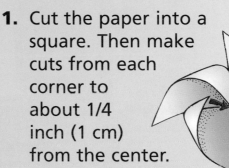

1. Cut the paper into a square. Then make cuts from each corner to about 1/4 inch (1 cm) from the center.
2. Take the left corner of each triangle and loop into the middle.
3. Put the bead on the pin.
4. Stick the pin through all four corners in the center.

5. Push the pin into the stick. Now blow on your pinwheel or hold it in the wind. What happens?

Change Is in the Air

Oxygen in the air mixes easily with some chemicals. This process is called **oxidation**. Fire is a product of oxidation. It occurs when oxygen combines with hot temperatures and a fuel source. The more oxygen there is in the air, the faster the fire will burn. Without oxygen, fire cannot burn. With a lot of oxygen, fire burns quickly.

The rust on an old car is also created by oxidation. Oxygen mixes with the car's metal. The metal turns into a red dust called rust.

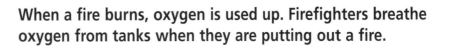

When a fire burns, oxygen is used up. Firefighters breathe oxygen from tanks when they are putting out a fire.

Some objects, such as cars, need to be protected from oxygen. Oxidation can destroy them. Paint protects the metal on cars. Valuable old books and wines are kept in special places that are free of oxygen. Apples and bananas have peels that protect the fruit inside. If an apple is left in the air after being peeled, it will turn brown.

The rust on an old car is an example of oxidation.

Air Pressure

Air has weight. It pushes down on us all the time. It also pushes at us from all sides, just as water does when we are swimming. This pushing is called air pressure. We do not feel this pushing. Our bodies push back with the same amount of pressure that air applies to us.

Water pressure is stronger than air pressure. Scuba equipment keeps the air pressure in the diver's lungs equal to the pressure of the water so the diver can breathe.

The air pressure in a ball allows it to keep its shape.

As you blow air into a balloon, it grows in size. Air inside the balloon takes up space. It pushes the sides of the balloon out. The balloon expands because the air pressure inside the balloon is stronger than the air pressure outside.

Activity

Make a Balloon Rocket

You need a balloon, a plastic straw, tape, string, and two chairs for this activity. Tie one end of the string to one of the chairs. Cut a piece of straw the length of your little finger. Put the string through the straw and tie the string to the other chair. Pull the chairs until the string is tight. Pull the straw to one end. Stick a loop of tape to the straw. Blow up the balloon, but do not tie it. Stick the balloon to the tape on the straw. Now release the balloon. The balloon and straw will travel along the string as air pressure is released.

A balloon's flexible body lets a lot of air into a small space. The sound you hear when a balloon pops is the sound of **pressurized** air escaping.

23

Flying

Birds and airplanes use air pressure to fly. Their wings have a special shape. Wings are flat on the bottom and rounded on top. When air moves over this shape, there is less air pressure above the wing than below it. This difference in air pressure causes the wings to lift.

Feathers help birds fly. The flat row of feathers at the front of a bird's wing allows air to flow smoothly over the top and bottom of the wing. Feathers at the wing tip "catch" air as the wing flaps down. This helps maintain the lift created by air pressure.

Trumpeter swans live in Canada and the northern United States in the summer and fly south in the winter. Their strong wings are designed to carry them over long distances.

Airplane wings do not move up and down like bird wings. They stay in one position. Most airplanes need to speed along the ground before they can fly. This builds up air pressure under the wings.

Helicopters use rotating wings called **propellers** to fly. Propellers are curved on top and flat underneath. The shape of the propellers helps create the lift needed to get off the ground.

Air moves over and under a helicopter's propellers. This gives it the air pressure needed to fly.

Puzzler

The first flying machine, or airplane, was designed hundreds of years ago. Flying machines appear in ancient myths and stories. But, did you know that helicopters were also thought of a long time ago? When was the first helicopter designed? Who designed it?

Answer: Leonardo Da Vinci, a great artist and inventor who lived in Italy from 1452-1519, designed the first helicopter. He also designed a flying machine, a construction crane, and many other machines.

Is Your Future Up in the Air?

Many people have jobs that involve air. Do any of these jobs interest you?

Hang gliding has become a popular sport in North America. People take classes from hang gliding instructors to learn how to handle the glider.

Airline pilots attend flight school to learn to fly aircraft safely. Pilots usually need 1,500 hours of flight time, or time spent flying a plane, before they can become airline pilots.

Helicopter pilots
fly people on tours.

They also rescue and fly sick and injured people to hospitals. Without helicopter pilots, many people would never be rescued from skiing and hiking accidents in remote or hard-to-reach areas.

Activity

Do Your Own Research

Ask a parent or teacher to help you find information about these air careers:

- air traffic controller
- aircraft technician
- environmentalist
- hang gliding instructor
- hot air balloonist
- meteorologist

Hot air balloonists
often work for companies.

Their balloons advertise the companies. Hot air balloonists also work in Africa and other countries. They take people up in balloons over the tops of national parks. People can see animals and other points of interest from above.

Pollution

Air pollution is waste that floats in the air. Gas, oil, and coal release dirt into the atmosphere when they burn. Humans burn a lot of gas, oil, and coal. **Smog** is visible air pollution. You can see smog over some cities. It appears as a yellow haze. Car exhaust is the main cause of smog.

Air pollution also causes acid rain. Water vapor mixes with air pollution and forms clouds. The rain that falls from these clouds contains acid. Acid rain can harm nature. It contributes to the death of trees and lakes.

Acid rain has caused damage to our forests and wildlife. Little things, such as riding a bicycle to work or school, can help reduce air pollution.

People can keep air clean by burning as little coal, gas, and oil as possible. Ask yourself the following questions about your house and family. Are you doing all you can to keep the air clean?

- Is your house drafty or well **insulated**? The draftier it is, the more fuel is burned to heat it.
- If your family has a car, do your parents drive the speed limit, or faster? Speeding burns more gas than driving slowly.
- How many times a day do people in your house drive, walk, or ride bikes?
- Is your house heated with coal, gas, oil, or another source? Some energy sources, such as wind and the Sun, are cleaner than coal, gas, and oil.

Weather centers in large cities, such as New York and Los Angeles, create smog reports so that people will know how much smog is in the air.

29

Air Play

If you have ever flown a kite, or hung up a windsock, you have played with air. Windsocks are tubes of thin plastic or cloth that are closed at one end. They are usually attached to a pole that is placed in the ground. When the wind blows, it fills the sock with air, and the sock swivels on the pole. The closed end of the sock will point to the direction in which the wind is blowing. Windsocks are used at airports to show the direction of the wind. They are fun to put up in your backyard, too.

Windsocks come in many shapes and colors and are used all over the world. These fish windsocks are from Japan.

Make a Kite

Make your own mini kite with two plastic straws, thread, tape, string, wrapping paper, and scissors. Ask an adult to help you with this project.

1. Cut one inch (2.5 centimeters) off one straw.
2. Tie the shorter straw to the longer one 1/4 way from the top to make a cross shape. Cut slits at the ends of each straw.
3. Wrap thread around the outside of the straws. Use the slits to hold the thread in place.
4. Trace the shape of your kite on the wrapping paper. Make the shape a little bit bigger than the frame of your kite. Cut out the shape. Tape the straws and thread to the paper.
5. Tie one more thread to the top and bottom of the long straw. Tie a long piece of string to the middle of this thread. This is the string you will hold.
6. Now make a tail. Tie little pieces of wrapping paper to a long piece of thread. Fasten this to the bottom of your kite.
7. Go outside and run with the kite behind you.

Be careful not to fly your kite near power lines or tall trees!

Glossary

atmosphere: the layers of gases around the Earth.

carbon dioxide: a gas formed by breathing.

evaporate: to change from a solid or liquid into a gas.

gravity: the force that pulls things toward Earth.

insulated: protected from heat, sound, or electricity.

lungs: the pair of air-breathing organs in humans and other animals.

oxidation: process in which oxygen mixes with chemicals.

oxygen: colorless, odorless gas needed to support life.

photosynthesis: the process by which plants use carbon dioxide, water, and sunlight to make food.

pressurize: to maintain a certain air pressure in a confined space.

propeller: rotating blades that provide force for movement.

smog: particles of pollution that form a haze in the air.

water vapor: water that is in the form of a gas.

windpipe: the tube leading from the mouth and nose to the lungs.

wind turbine: tall towers that create electricity from wind power.

Index

Web Sites

www.ohio.com/kr/blimp/blimp.htm

www.fatlion.com/science/airpressure.html

www.hhmi.org/coolscience/airjunk/

imagerystudios.com/sk/clean1.htm

Some web sites stay current longer than others. For further web sites, use your search engines to locate the following topics: *atmosphere, flight, humidity,* and *wind power.*